Triad Interloc

by Marilyn Doheny

All Rights Reserved Copyright ©1991 Doheny Publications

Art direction, Graphic Design
and Illustrations: C. Eng Design
Photography: Mark Frey

FABRIC SELECTION

1. Select a wide assortment of fabrics to begin.

2. You will need between 10 to 70 fabrics depending on the project selected (see **Yardage Chart** below).

3. Be sure to have *all values* represented: darks, mediums and lights.

4. Be sure to include *all sizes* of print scale: large, medium and small. Don't forget to use solids too!

5. Separate the fabrics that you have selected into three catagories:

Theme fabrics	wider cut widths (2¼″ – 4″)
Filler fabrics	medium cut widths (1¼″ – 2″)
Accent fabrics	narrow cut widths (¾″ – 1″)

A balanced Triad Interlock with random extensions

YARDAGE CHART

Quilt Style†	Theme Fabrics	Filler Fabrics	Accent Fabrics	Background Fabric
Wall (sm. square)	4 fabrics ⅛ yd ea	6 fabrics ⅛ yd ea	4 fabrics ⅛ yd ea	½ yd
Wall (sm. rectangle)	6 fabrics ¼ yd ea	6 fabrics ¼ yd ea	6 fabrics ⅛ yd ea	½ yd
Lap (45″ x 60″)	6 fabrics ⅓ yd ea	6 fabrics ¼ yd ea	8 fabrics ⅛ yd ea	1 yd
Twin (60″ x 90″)	6 fabrics ½ yd ea	6 fabrics ⅓ yd ea	8 fabrics ¼ yd ea	2 yd
Double (90″ x 90″)	7 fabrics ⅔ yd ea	7 fabrics ½ yd ea	10 fabrics ⅓ yd ea	2 yd
Queen (100″ x 100″)	7 fabrics ⅔ yd ea	7 fabrics ½ yd ea	10 fabrics ⅓ yd ea	2½ yd
King (110″ x 110″)	8 fabrics 1 yd ea	7 fabrics ⅔ yd ea	10 fabrics ⅓ yd ea	2½ yd
Triad Sampler (12 Individual Triads)	16 fabrics ⅛ yd ea	24 fabrics ⅛ yd ea	12 fabrics ⅛ yd ea	3 yds
Hexagon Triad Sampler (8 hexagonal Triads)	24 fabrics ⅓ yd ea	24 fabrics ¼ yd ea	16 fabrics ⅛ yd ea	3 yds

† Actual quilt sizes and background fabric requirements will vary according to Triad pattern development.

Acknowledgments: I want to thank every talented quilter/friend who worked with me in the 12 Month Series and submitted their quilts for photographic consideration in this book. It was a delight as well as a difficulty to narrow the field from all of the wonderful choices. A special congratulations to the four generous quilters whose work was selected to feature the Triad Interlock pattern variations—take a bow!

T his elaborate interlocking pattern is achieved by using equilateral triangles that come from at least three different strata units. The more irregular and contrasting that each of the strata units are, the more complex and intriguing the effect. The top and bottom edge of each strata unit contribute two different looking triangles (Figures 1A & B). When three strata units are created, six different looking triangles emerge. Three of the six triangle styles are selected for the basic Interlock and the remaining three triangle styles are used to create the extension arms of the interlocking design.

HIGH CONTRAST GUIDELINES

It is best to use at least three different strata combinations together rather than one strata plan repeatedly. With larger quilts it is desirable to make 4 to 6 different strata units. There should be enough of these strata units so that sufficient numbers of triangles can be cut from each unit style.

It is necessary to create each of the strata units with high-contrast fabric relationships. This means that fabrics having high contrast: a) values, b) colors, c) print textures, and d) cut widths, are sewn side by side to create one strata unit. Then another high contrast strata unit is designed and created. Each strata unit must be the same height after sewing and there must be a minimum of three different strata units (Figure 1B).

It is essential that all of the strata units in a project have the same sewn height—the *exact sewn and ironed height.* Any strata height can be utilized but once selected, it must remain a constant measurement for all strata units in that project. The specific information in this text refers to strata units that are 6″ tall when sewn and ironed. All strata units are expected to be 40″– 45″ long.

The exact number of triangles required depends on the extent of the "Triad set" designed using the triangles. Each strata which is 6″ tall will provide 11 to 12 triangles that are a wonderful scale for wall, lap and twin bed quilt pattern development. **Chart E** gives you "yield guidelines" for strata units that are other than 6″ tall. This will assist you in determining yardage and strata requirements for miniature Triad work as well as Double, Queen and King-size projects.

Figure 1A

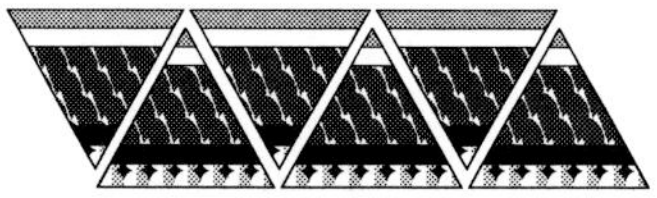

Figure 1B

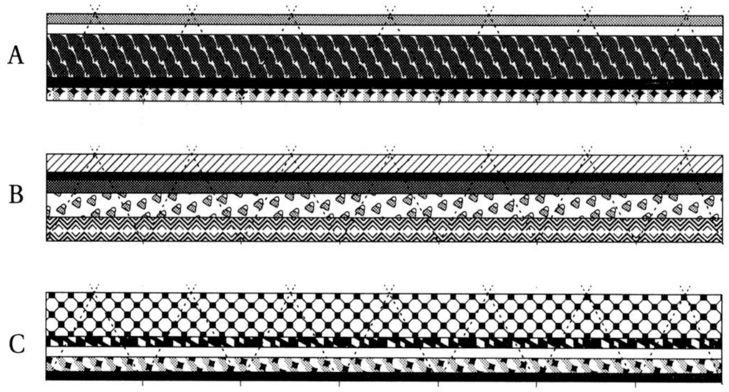

FABRIC PREPARATION

Minimum Strata Production

Plan, cut and sew strips together to create three very different 6″ x 45″ strata units. Assorted 6″ strata combinations are provided in **Chart B**.

The example shows how to determine (or plan) a strata height.

1. The finished size is written for each strip width.
2. When the widths of the individual strips total 5½″, a 6″ strata has been planned.

NOTE: Each outside strip still has *one* of its 1/4″ seam areas unsewn which contributes to the actual strata height.

For example:

Final Height	Cut Width (½″ more)
½″	1″
½″	1″
3″	3½″
½″	1″
1″	1½″
5½″	

+½″ extra for outside edge (top and bottom strip) that have not yet lost their last 1/4″.

6″ tall

CHART B—Assorted 6″ strata height combinations

Any arrangements of these cut sizes *within a plan* will work. Rearrange the order when sewing for additional effects. Never put a 3/4″ cut strip at the outside edge of a strata plan.

Cut Size Combinations (inches)							
A	**B**	**C**	**D**	**E**	**F**	**G**	**H**
1	1¾	3½	2	4	3	1½	2
1	¾	1	1	1	1½	¾	¾
3½	1¼	1	1	1	2½	1	2
1	2½	¾	1	1½		¾	1
1½	2½	1¾	1			2½	2¼
			1½			1½	
			1½			1	

For larger quilts, always create *at least* two identical strata units for every strata created.

ALTERNATE IDEAS

1. For all other strata heights you will need to create your own combinations.
2. Be sure to allow for the actual unsewn 1/4″ seam allowances on each edge (see example above). They contribute an extra 1/2″ to the actual strata height.
3. It is assumed that 1/4″ seams are taken. If you take hardy or slight 1/4″ seams, be sure to allow for this in your calculations. Strata units with five seams will alter differently than strata units with only three seams.
4. Use high contrast fabric selection guidelines.
5. *Have 1 yard of background fabric as a minimum.*
6. You may wish to select background fabrics after the Triad Interlock design is established. This allows the design "to talk to you" first.

REMINDER: Whatever strata height is created for a Triad Interlock project, *all of the strata units for that project must be the same height.* The entire "set" within a quilt depends upon equilateral triangles that have a consistent size. **Be sure to measure** every strata unit after it is created and trim or add on as needed to get a uniform height for all of the strata units involved. *Do not assume that your planning and sewing* will generate a 6″ tall unit or consistent units. Measure to be sure and adjust as necessary to be consistent. A different number of seams equals a different distortion factor!

RULE: a) Tall fabric units yield fewer triangles. Narrow fabric units yield more triangles.

b) Tall fabric units yield larger triangles. Narrow fabric units yield smaller triangles.

Use the **Chart E** to plan your strata size and triangle yield if it is other than 6″.

CHART C				
Quilt Size	**Strata Height**	**Strata Volume**		
	Choose one per project	No.of *different* strata units	No.of each strata to be created	Total No.of strata units for project
Wall Small	4″, 5″ or 6″	3	1	3
Wall Rectangle	4″, 5″ or 6″	3	2	6
Lap	6″ or 7″	4	3	12
Twin	6″, 7″ or 8″	4	4	16
Double	7″ or 8″	5	5	25
Queen	8″, 9″ or 10″	5	6	30
King	8″, 9″ or 10″	6	6	36
Triad Sampler (12 Individual Triads)	6″	6	1	6
Hexagonal Sampler (Hexagon Triads)	6″	6	3	18

Chart D
CHECK AND CORRECT

It is possible that the strata units that you have created are not perfect. But this does not mean that they are not useful! It simply means that they need a bit of extra help. It is important to eliminate distortions as soon as they appear. The trick is in learning what the distortions are, how to correct each of them, and how to get back on track with the quilt construction.

First of all, you want to check that you have even, consistent widths of *each* fabric strip running the entire length of the strata unit. You also want to have an overall "straight" strata unit. Many things can contribute to the distortions during each of the cutting and sewing sequences.

1. If you have seam work that is causing irregular widths, now is the time to correct it before proceeding with any counter-cutting. They can be attributable to: a) poor cutting consistency, b) poor ironing, or c) improperly taken seam allowances.

a) If the distortion is due to poor ironing, then re-iron the strata to remedy "accordion pleating." Grasp the width of the strata and pull it apart to check for popping. If needed, re-iron and proceed on. The strata should be as tall, flat and wide as possible.

b) If the problem is due to poor cutting consistency, unfortunately nothing can be changed at this point. The cuts are real—they are done. Replace the strip(s) with correctly cut strips.

c) If the distortion is due to improperly taken seam allowances, then simply redo the seam from the backside. This can either be done by taking the seam allowance larger, or by removing it and taking less of an allowance. Be sure to re-iron before counter-cutting.

2. You may have strata distortions that look like lettuce leaf edges or like a small rainbow arch. These can be "worked around." As you work through the counter-cutting sequences, you will continually cut away any distortion while constantly maintaining a 60° angle at the strata end.

Check and Correct

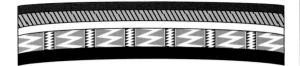

Narrow/Wide Channel Distortion
Adjust seams to be consistent before
counter-cutting

"Rainbow" Distortion
It will be necessary to maintain the 60° angle after
each diamond is cut. Trim off the strata distortion
before cutting the next diamond.

1. Sew the strips together. *Check and Correct* as necessary.

2. When sewing, don't pull on the fabric strip. This will help eliminate several problems before they develop.

3. Iron to its full height. Seam allowances must be flat. If two strata are identical, iron one up and one down.

4. Establish a beginning 90° angle at one end of the unit using an internal seam to gauge the angle. *In a strata unit, the least disturbed seams are near the center.*

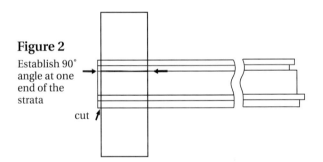

Figure 2
Establish 90°
angle at one
end of the
strata

cut

To do this: Clean up the beginning end to 90° (Figure 2). Do not omit this step! NOTE: For str*ata it is essential to use an internal seam as the guide for establishing any angle.* Do not use a fabric at the edge of a strata unit—all internal distortions are reflected at the edges of a strata. It is not a "true" point from which to guide counter-cuts. A strata unit is analogous to a lake where every seam, like a water skier or swimmer, can potentially cause a rippling disturbance. These distortions accumulate at the *edge* of the strata as they do along the shore of a lake. The "calmest" area of both is the center.

5. Using the same internal seam, establish a full 60° angle at the beginning end (Fig. 3A). **To do this:** Select one of the lines running through the 60° "button" of an Omnigrid™ Ruler and place it on an internal seam. The long outside edge of the ruler will be running across the strata unit at 60°. Slide the ruler edge into position to make a full 60° cut.

Figure 3A

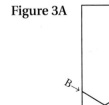

B→
A→

Select one of
the lines running
through the
60° button

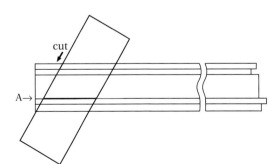

cut

A→

6. Cut the entire strata unit into 60° diamonds 6″ wide. If your strata is 6″ tall, the counter-cuts *must be* the same distance wide as the strata is tall. Use the strata unit height to determine the width of the counter-cut (Figure 3B). I call these "square" diamonds. This measurement is not made along the outside edge of the diamond. It is an internal, *parallel "wall to wall" measurement.* Always maintain a 60° strata end (see **Chart D—Check and Correct**). Clean up and redefine the 60° angle as necessary. If your strata has "lettuce leaf edges" or a "rainbow arch," you will *clean up* the 60° angle after every diamond is cut, before cutting the next diamond (Figure 3C).

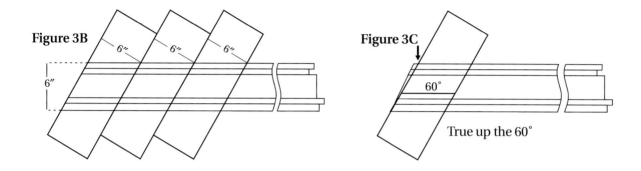

Figure 3B

Figure 3C

True up the 60°

7. Counter-cut all of the diamonds on their elbow to elbow diagonal (Figure 4 and 5).

8. **Trim 1/4″ off the base of each triangle.** Be sure to trim from the base the edge which is parallel to the internal seams (Figure 6).

NOTE: This is an **essential trim** in order for "opposing angle" seams to match later when sewing triangles back together. Even though it might not make sense to you to do this process, *just do it for now—it is essential.*

REMINDER: *Do not* trim before releasing the diamond into two triangles. It is imperative that you keep the 1/4″ tip area of each alternate triangle intact (Figure 6).

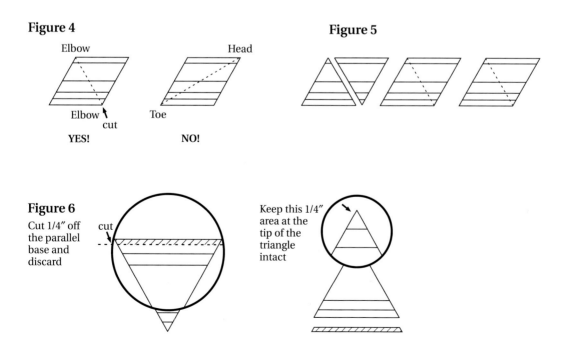

Figure 4

Elbow

Head

Elbow   cut

Toe

YES!   **NO!**

Figure 5

Figure 6

Cut 1/4″ off the parallel base and discard

cut

Keep this 1/4″ area at the tip of the triangle intact

Figure 7

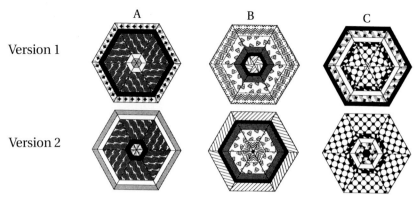

Version 1

Version 2

9. Each strata unit contributes two different triangles – those off the top edge and those off the bottom. Use each group independently and create 6 different "plates." Use six identical triangles to form a hexagon plate. Do this for each strata unit created (Fig. 7). NOTE: If only five identical triangles are available, use them. Five will also work due to the "Swiss Cheese Factor" of pattern development (see step 11).

10. Select three of your favorite plates— one from each strata pair to start. You are looking for high contrast and crisply defined differences between the three plates selected. They will form the basic Triad Interlock. Nestle them together (Figure 8A).

Figure 8A   **Figure 8B**

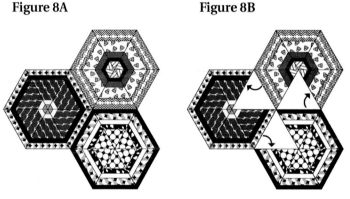

11. Notice that in the nestled area of the three different hexagonal plates, there exists another hexagonal area. It is composed of a *pair of triangles* from each of the three plates. In a "Swiss Cheese" fashion, remove one triangle from each pair (Figure 8B).

12. To create the Interlock, extension arms need to be developed.
To do this: Pretend that each of the remaining triangles has a "hinge" where you see the small dark spot "•." Pretend that this "•" area of the triangle is a*nchored* but is *free to rotate*. Now rotate each one of the three triangles, one at a time, while keeping each of the "•" corners anchored. Follow the arrows for rotation direction.
    A) The arrow of triangle #2 rotates the triangle into space #1. Notice that the external fabric of the hexagon remains continuous on the outside area of the hexagon and also becomes the extension arm via rotation (Figure 9).
    B) Rotate triangle #4 into the empty space of #3. Check that the external fabric of the hexagon creates an extension effect.
    C) Rotate triangle #6 into the empty space of #5. Check that your creation (rotation) has the same continuity and orderly arm extension of Figure 10A.
This arm extension creates the basic Triad Interlock. It is essential to establish a connectedness or piercing interlock of the three hexagonal plates.

13. Select one triangle each from the *unused* (opposite) plates. Use these triangles to "fill in" and create the connectedness (complete pattern) of each arm extension. Check your creation for proper placement and positioning against Figure 10B. This Triad Interlock is the beginning as well as the basic foundation for all remaining pattern development. It should be very crisp and visually defined by a full Triad.

NOTE: If one of the three units in the Triad blurs into another unit, then replace it in the layout with its opposite counterpart. Continue to do this until you are happy with a visually clean and defined Triad effect.

At this stage, you have made one individual Triad. You can stop the pattern development here, or you can make several more of these individual Triads for a sampler of Triads floating on a background of cloth. (See background fabric cutting and row assembly sections.)

No inset piecing is required for the any of the Triad designs. See Background Triangle Cutting information to determine the correct size of your background triangle.

Figure 9

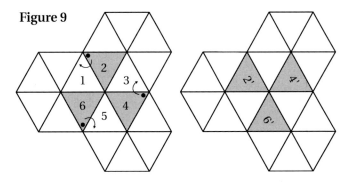

Figure 10A

Figure 10B

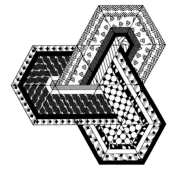

14. If you wish to continue with pattern development, there are several simple, balanced and logical ways to continue to add triangles to increase the Interlock as well as random and spontaneous extensions that are fun! Play around with each idea until you are happy with the effects of *your* triangles. It is possible to create additional strata units at any time if more triangles are desired. These new strata units do not need to look like any of the previous strata units. They only need to have the same strata height.

A. Hexagonal "Paperclip"   D. Balanced/Irregular
B. Short arm extension   E. Random Fun
C. Long arm extension

After the design has been achieved, then background triangles can be cut and added to fill in the necessary missing areas.

If background triangles are cut from plain strips of cloth rather than strata units, the plain strip should be cut 1/4″ smaller (or more narrow), than the height of the strata units in the design. Counter-cut into diamonds 1/4″ smaller as well.
NOTE: **Do not trim the 1/4″ from each base,** it is not necessary when no internal seam needs to be realigned.

For example: To cut 60° diamonds from the background fabric. The cut size of the strip should be 1/4″ less than the strata height. For example: if the strata height is 6″ then the background strip will be 5¾″. *Be sure to counter-cut at 5¾″ as well.*

Figure 11

Figure 12

15. Counter-cut all necessary diamonds on their short diagonal to create the required triangles as previously indicated. Place them into the pattern to fill out the edges of the entire unit (Figure 11).

16. Sew the triangles together, row by row, on the diagonal (Figure 12).

17. As the triangles are sewn together, it will be necessary to create perfect seam junctions (Figure 13). There are three types of junctions between triangles that you will encounter: a) *non-related seams*, b) *obvious* and, c) *internal*.

18. The *non-related* triangle scams are exactly that—non-related. They are easy (Figure 14).

Figure 13

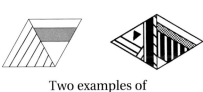

Detail

Figure 14

Two examples of
non-related triangles

Figure 15A

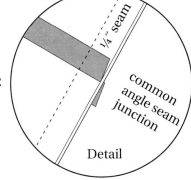

Figure 15B

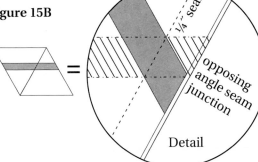

19. The *obvious* seam junctions interact like "back door neighbors sharing a secret." This pair of triangles "pivot" after being sewn. These seam crossings are convenient—they happen at the edge. They are easy to create by interlocking at the edge of the seam being taken (Figure 15A).

20. Opposing angle seam junctions are created *internally,* 1/4″ inward from the edge as their seams cross one another at an angle. These are more difficult to navigate as nothing nestles together (Figure 15B). This pair of triangles will have a "continuous seam look" after being sewn. They are fussy to get right!

21. Bind as desired or continue to add additional borders.

Remember: If you are not having fun…you are not doing it right!

SAMPLES OF THE 1990's

A collection of individual Triads would make a beautiful sampler quilt. It is also possible to continue to "add on" more interlocking appendages as desired. This can be done on graph paper first if you wish to tally the necessary number of triangles that each type of strata must yield. It may be necessary to create several identical strata units

Figure 16

Long Arm Extensions

Figure 16B

Short Arm Extensions

Figure 16C

Hexagonal Sampler

Figure 17

to get the proper number of identical triangles for the design that you prefer. Simply creating some triangles and playing around with them is a useful method for exploring design possibilities. Don't overlook that children can design with these wonderful triangles after you have made them. View the additional illustrated "sets" to inspire your creativity. You may wish to create "new" strata that is different than the three originally designed. All of this is possible and desirable. Triad Interlock is full of *pattern development potential!*

Extended Triad Interlock uses extension triangles that are "specific." They are related to the basic strata used in the center areas of the Triad Interlock (Figure 16).

Balanced Interlock uses extension triangles that create a full symmetrical balance. The triangles can be extensions to those used in the basic Triad or they can be from entirely new strata combinations (see example on page 1).

Random Interlock Additions at will! (Figure 17)
NOTE: *Darker* triangles will appear further away, *lighter* triangles will appear closer— *one strata can produce both.* Each of the strata edges must concentrate on opposite values. It may be useful (and fun) to use the illusion of depth for secondary developments within the pattern. However, it is not necessary to consider values to achieve the Triad Interlock design.

For preplanning your strata requirements for any strata height, use the following chart combined with our specialty Triad Interlock graph paper.

Chart E will help you plan:

A) the necessary number of strata units in advance for any design.

B) the size of your quilt design based upon strata height.

base

height

CHART E			
Strata Height sewn + ironed	**Approx. number of** triangles per strata unit (May yield one extra)	**Size of Triangles** based on true 4″ seam allowance margins*	
		Base	Height
4″	14	3½	3
5″	12	4⅝	4
6″	10	5¾	5
7″	8	6⅞	6
8″	8	8	7
9″	6	9¼	8
10″	6	10¼	9

* whatever the actual strata height, all strata must be identical and the counter-cut width must be the same in order to create equilateral triangles. For example: a 7¼″ tall strata unit would be counter-cut at 7¼″ wide (two rulers side by side would be required to attain this width. A 6″ ruler cannot be used.

Use **Chart E** with the graph paper available for Triad Interlock Design. Graph paper for this and other *Strata Art Quilt Designs* is available from Doheny Publications – $4.95 plus $1.50 shipping and handling.

About the Author

Marilyn has always been both a people person and a fabric person. She started making quilts in 1982. The first of her three children was then nine months old, and she desperately needed an outlet with lots of adult interaction. So, to save her sanity and work with fabric, she enrolled in a six-week basic quilting course. During the entire six weeks, each student attempted to piece one pinwheel potholder using a single triangle template, then quilt it, and bind it. Truly, great things come from humble beginnings. Marilyn never finished that potholder (although it does hang, "in progress," on her sewing room wall). She was hooked and began to search the public libraries for books of quilt patterns. She then discovered that there are shapes other than triangles and was suddenly and overwhelmingly in love with the endless possibilities!

Since then, Marilyn's life has included every aspect of quiltmaking, from creating her own quilts to teaching others about the art. With joy and enthusiasm she has made hundreds of quilt tops and has inspired and instructed others to do the same. Marilyn is always dreaming up new patterns and inventing innovative sewing techniques for the traditional favorites. Her quilter's world is full of artistic achievements that "piece together" and give purpose to the joys of her life: color, texture, fabric, geometric patterns and people.

Other quality products from **Cutting Edge Quilt Designs**™ and **Doheny Publications**.
Available at your local quilt store, or write to us at: P.O. Box 25151, Seattle, WA 98125

45° Kaleidoscope Wedge Ruler $16.96
Create clever, magical Kaleidoscope illusions fast and easily with this superb tool! Includes complete instructions with quick quilt pattern.

9° Circle Wedge Ruler $18.95
Infinite circular designs! Innovative new ruler includes instructions for 20 different patterns. Create spectacular quilts or clothing embellishments.

■ PATTERN BOOKLETS
featuring Marilyn Doheny's Rotary Magic© techniques for perfect cutting without templates

Amish Sparkle Star $6.95
A delightful interpretation of a traditional Amish pieced pattern.

Maple Leaves $6.95
Falling leaves is the motif of this wonderfully soothing quilt. Use up to 175 different fabrics for these 25 leaves — a great scrap quilt opportunity!

Trailing Vines $6.95
A glorious scrap quilt inspired by Susan McCord's antique quilt (1846), in the collection of the Henry Ford Museum. For hand or machine applique. Sections of the design can be used for clothing embellishments as well.

■ OTHER PATTERN BOOKLETS
Canadian Geese $7.95
Stunning, award-winning 52" quilt featuring two majestic Canadian Geese. Complete paper patch applique instructions.

Reticule $7.95
Original design of a "country lady's purse" used by women in the early 19th century to transport needle work projects. You will be delighted with its charming appearance as well as its remarkable usefulness. Quick and easy to sew. Includes instructions for three sizes.

Feathered Wishbone $4.95
Six versatile fine hand quilting motifs for blocks and borders

■ BOOKS
And if you enjoyed this book, other new titles from the **Strata Art Series—** *For Contemporary Eyes Only!* are:
Cubic Pinwheels $10.95
Cubic Ribbons $10.95
Triad Interlock $10.95
Woven Ribbons $10.95

Goosey Hearts $14.95
A lavishly illustrated 64-page book of original applique and hand quilting patterns featuring a full size fold-out of the Goosey Hearts quilt (38" x 28").

■ DESIGN ACCESSORIES
Kaleidoscope Design Grid $4.95
Graph paper featuring 4 and 6 division wedges for use with the 45° Kaleidoscope Ruler.

9° Circle Design Grid $4.95
The perfect accessory for designing elaborate spiral motion patterns for the 9° Circle Wedge Ruler.

Graph paper for the *Strata Art Series*
Triad Interlock Design Grid $4.95
Cubic Pinwheels Design Grid $4.95
Cubic Ribbons Design Grid $4.95
Woven Ribbons Design Grid $4.95

■ ROTARY CUTTING EQUIPMENT
Omnigrid™ **Ruler**   3" x 18" $8.95
                          6" x 24" $12.95
Olfa® Rotary Cutter (large) $15.95
Replacement blades (bulk 10) $36.00
Cutting Mat   medium $21.50
                  large $39.00

Please send orders to:
Cutting Edge Quilt Designs™
P.O. Box 25151
Seattle, WA 98125

Include $1.50 shipping and handling for paper products;
$2.50 for rulers and cutting mats

Wholesale inquiries welcome.
Prices subject to change without notice.